The Craziest Riddle Book in the World

▼ ▼ ▼ ▼ ▼ ▼ ▼ ▼ ▼ ▼ ▼ ▼ ▼

The Craziest Riddle Book in the World

▼ ▼ ▼ ▼ ▼ ▼ ▼ ▼ ▼ ▼ ▼ ▼

Lori Miller Fox

Illustrations by
Sanford Hoffman

STERLING PUBLISHING CO., INC.
New York

To my husband Charlie for his never-ending love, constant support, and infinite patience.

Library of Congress Cataloging-in-Publication Data Available

10   9   8   7   6   5   4   3   2   1

Published in 2004 by Sterling Publishing Co., Inc.
387 Park Avenue South
New York, NY 10016
Based on the previously published *The Craziest Riddle Book in the World* by Lori Miller Fox
© 1991 by Lori Miller Fox
Distributed in Canada by Sterling Publishing
^{c}/o Canadian Manda Group
One Atlantic Avenue, Suite 105
Toronto, Ontario, M6K 3E7, Canada
Distributed in Great Britain and Europe by Chris Lloyd at
Orca Book Services
Stanley House, Fleets Lane, Poole BH15 3AJ, England
Distributed in Australia by Capricorn Link (Australia) Pty Ltd.
P.O. Box 704, Windsor, NSW 2756, Australia

Sterling ISBN 1-4027-0898-X

Contents

▼ ▼ ▼ ▼ ▼ ▼ ▼ ▼
▼

1.
Wacky Warm-ups

▼ ▼

What do jigsaw puzzles do when they get bad news?

Go to pieces.

What ice cream do monkeys eat?

Chocolate chimp.

What do archaeologists dig up at baboon burial grounds?

Ba-bones.

Who helped the werewolf go to the ball?
Its Hairy Godmother.

What do members of the Scooby Doo fan club pay?
Scooby dues.

Who is Scooby Doo's evil twin?
Scooby Don't.

What two-ton animal can put you in a trance?
A hypnopotamus.

Why did the mother horse scold her little colt?
For misbehooving.

How do baby birds know how to fly?
They just wing it.

What did the parrot say to the streetcar?
"Trolley want a cracker?"

Why did the chicken cross the amusement park?
To get to the other ride.

What's the difference between a lollipop and a chicken?
One you suck and one you pluck.

Where do fish go to get a degree?
To tuna-versities.

How do loudmouths pay for college?
They get hollerships.

What do mechanics do in aerobics class?
Touch their tow trucks.

How do you hit slime?
With a sludgehammer.

How do you measure an aardvark?
   With an aardstick.

What do you call an unidentified flying cow?
   A Moo-F-O.

What star slept for 100 years?
   Rip Van Twinkle.

Who delivers trees overnight?
Federal Exspruce.

Where do dead letters go?
To the Ghost Office.

SILLY SUBSCRIPTIONS

What's a frog's favorite magazine?
Warts Illustrated.

What's a lawyer's favorite
magazine?
Courts Illustrated.

What's a clothing manufacturer's
favorite magazine?
Shorts Illustrated.

Where do customers trade merchandise?
In swapping malls.

If you buy doughnuts by the dozen, how do
you buy bees?
By the buzzin'.

What would you get if you crossed an alligator with a pickle?
A crocodill.

What long-necked bird can't be seen?
Casper the Friendly Goose.

What's the difference between an informer in jail and a monkey in the zoo?
One sings behind bars, the other swings behind bars.

What's Santa's background?
North Polish.

Why was Santa's Little Helper depressed?
He had low elf-esteem.

How does Santa communicate in Morse code?
With dots and Dashers.

2.

Feature Creatures

Where did animals play video games during the Great Flood?

In Noah's Arc-ade.

What's the difference between a lizard, a crybaby, and the Roadrunner?

One creeps, one weeps, and one beeps.

Why did the amoeba take two aspirins?

Its head was splitting.

What animals can survive the coldest weather?
Polar brrrrs.

What bear never bathes?
Winnie-the-Pew.

What bears live in Tokyo?
Japan-da bears.

What dog is always smiling?
Grin Tin Tin.

Where does Santa's dog paddle?
In the North Pool.

What tricks can you teach a dog in a beauty parlor?
To comb, set, and roller over.

What would you get if you crossed a beautician with a dog?
A shampoodle.

What do you lend to a needy vet?
A helping hound.

What does a vet keep outside his front door?

A welcome mutt.

Where do smart dogs refuse to shop?

At flea markets.

How do cats confide in each other?

They purr their hearts out.

What scatterbrained creature climbed up the water spout?

The itsy ditzy spider.

What insect is hardest to understand?
A mumble bee.

What do you hear when you dial a
talkative bee?
A buzzy signal.

What do counselors lead at bee camp?
Sting-alongs.

What kills flies by sitting on them?
A fly squatter.

How do you revive a butterfly that has fainted?
With moth-to-moth resuscitation.

What does a crazy butterfly come out of?
A kook-oon.

What has many legs, antennae, and a sack of toys over its shoulder?
A Santa-pede.

What did Scrooge's sheep say to the mosquito at Christmas?
"Baaaa-humbug."

Why did the lamb go out in the middle of the night?
It was sheep walking.

How did the shepherd's flock look?
Sheepshape.

What nursery rhyme character is half elephant and half lamb?
Babar Black Sheep.

What do you get when an elephant sits on a squash?
Squish.

What did the mother groundhog say to her baby on Groundhog's Day?
"Gopher it!"

What animal hangs around caves and wins spelling bees?

An alpha-bat.

What snake builds things?

A boa constructor.

What poisonous snake is most spoiled by its parents?

A brattlesnake.

What lizard eats lots of lettuce?

A salad-mander.

What's a boring lizard called?
A crocodull.

What happens when you try to recognize sea mammals?
You can't tell one from the otter.

What does Charlie Tuna get from his admirers?
Fin mail.

DID YOU HEAR?

Did you hear the one about the owl?
Yes, it was a hoot.

Did you hear the one about the wolf?
Yes, it made me howl.

Did you hear the one about the lion?
Yes, it made me roar.

Did you hear the one about the skunk?
Yes, it stunk.

What did the big bird say to the little bird?
"You're a chirp off the old flock."

What would you get if you crossed an owl
with Santa Claus?
A bird that says, "Whooo whooo whooo."

What did the decorater put on the ocean
floor?
Whale-to-whale carpeting.

What do roosters pay when they join clubs?
Cock-a-doodle dues.

What would you get if you crossed a chicken with a cow?

Roost beef.

What would you get if you crossed a cow with Bullwinkle?

A moooose.

What naughty cow jumps off buildings for fun?

A dairy devil.

What do you say when choosing a cow?

"Eenie, meenie, miney, moo . . ."

What's the phone company's favorite Christmas song?

"Jingle Bills."

What did the doctor order when the bull broke its leg?

An ox-ray.

What would you get if you crossed oxen with zebras?

Steers and stripes.

How did the Three Little Pigs know the Big Bad Wolf was mad?

He left in a huff.

What did Bambi put on the back of his car?

A Thumper sticker.

What would you get if you crossed a hippo with a rodent?

A hippopota-mouse.

What sizes do skunks come in?

Large, medium, and smell.

Why did the little skunk listen to the big skunk?

Because it was odor and wiser.

Was that a rabbit I saw?

No, it was a hoptical illusion.

What do you call a smelly animal with purple hair?

A skunk rocker.

What would you get if you crossed a hippo with a rabbit?

A hop-popotamus.

3.
What's Cooking?

▼ ▼

Where do you buy food for dinner?
In a suppermarket

What's the difference between a diet and a crowded elevator?
One is hard to go on and one is hard to get off.

What happens when you add detergent to chicken noodle soup?
It becomes chicken noodle soap.

What's the difference between Peter Pan and a child who refuses to eat liver?

One doesn't want to grow up, and the other doesn't want to throw up.

What type of homework is assigned in chef's school?

Cookbook reports.

How do lions like their meat cooked? *Medium ROAR!*

What fast food can't stop talking?

A Big Yak.

How do straight-A students like their meat cooked?

Well done.

What's the most popular fast food in Italy?

Big Mac-aroni.

What does a frog order at a fast food restaurant?

A burger and flies.

What's Pinocchio's favorite dessert?
Chocolate liar cake.

What sort of dog loves cream cheese?
A puppyseed beagle.

Why did the baker insult the bread?
To get a rise out of it.

What vegetables always get extra special attention?
V. I. Peas.

What do you say when choosing vegetables?
"Zucchini, meenie, miney, moe . . ."

What does a lima bean wear on its head?
A lima beanie.

What is the difference between a baby and a cucumber?
One is tickled, the other is pickled.

What fairy tale tells the story of an unattractive wonton that becomes beautiful?
The Ugly Dumpling.

If you make hamburgers from ground beef, what do you make pork burgers from?
Groundhogs.

What do you say when choosing a hot dog?
"Weenie, meenie, miney, moe . . ."

Where are mashed potatoes buried?
In gravy yards.

What do successful people feed their dogs?
Yuppie Chow.

What decaffeinated coffee did they serve on the Titanic?
Sanka.

What do salad makers do while they sleep?
Toss and turn.

What dressing does Robinson Crusoe put on his salad?
Thousand Island.

What would you get if you crossed a tomato, some cheese, and a mail carrier?
A pizza that delivers itself.

Where do tiny macaroni and itty-bitty meatballs come from?
Little Italy.

What dish is served in Italy on New Year's Eve?
Confetti and meatballs.

What has cheese and pepperoni and can predict the future?
E. S. Pizza.

Why do waiters make good soldiers?
They're used to taking orders.

DID YOU HEAR?

Did you hear the one about the tomato?
Yes, it was rotten.

Did you hear the one about the cracker?
Yes, it was crumb-y.

Did you hear the one about the onion?
Yes, I laughed so hard I cried.

Did you hear the one about the hard-boiled egg?
Yes, it cracked me up.

What do traitors order for breakfast?
Eggs Benedict Arnold.

How do librarians file melted
marshmallows?
According to the Gooey Decimal System.

What does a vegetarian's car run on?
Aspara-gas.

4.

Crazy Careers

▼ ▼

What does a snake charmer wear around his neck?
A boa tie.

What kind of shoes do gas station attendants wear with dresses?
Pumps.

Why are locksmiths such good singers?
They're always in key.

What does Sherlock Holmes read for fun?
The ency-clue-pedia.

What do police learn in school?
How to tell crime.

What's the difference between a hotel clerk and a detective?
One checks people in, the other checks people out.

What's the difference between a pilot and a carpenter?
One boards planes, the other planes boards.

What's the difference between a deep thinker and an explorer?
One wonders, the other wanders.

If babysitters get paid by the hour, how do florists get paid?
By the flower.

Who can make popcorn and compose music at the same time?
Orville Redden-bach.

Do composers write long letters?
No, they write short notes.

Who was the most spoiled artist?
Rem-brat.

What's the dirtiest planet in the solar system?
Polluto.

What do you call thieves who steal only windshield wipers?
Windshield swipers.

How do Bullwinkle and his wife sign in at a hotel?
As Mister and Mooses.

What are a banker's favorite vowels?
I-O-U.

How did the sailor get married?
He tied the knot.

DID YOU HEAR?

Did you hear the one about
Napoleon?
Yes, it was historical.

Did you hear the one about the
tailor?
Yes, it had me in stitches.

Did you hear the one about the
amnesia patient?
Yes, but I forgot how it went.

Did you hear the one about the
caveman?
Yes, ages ago.

Who married the Jolly Green Giant and his wife?

A Justice of the Peas.

What did Santa's elves do in aerobics class?

They touched their mistle-toes.

What does a tailor use to repair a flat tire?

A needle and tread.

What lion was queen of Egypt?
  Leo-patra.

Who is the nastiest Disney character?
  Meanie Mouse.

What was Old MacDonald's nickname when
he was in the army?
  G-I-G-I-Joe.

What would you get if you crossed a dentist
with a military officer?
  A drill sergeant.

What would you get if you crossed Betty Crocker with Old Man Winter?
A baker who frosts windows.

What did one coal worker say to the other?
"Mine your own business."

What do astronauts carry on their ships in the winter?
Space heaters.

What herring ruled Russia?
The czar-dine.

What do authors have when they're too
nervous to write?
   Page fright.

Is he a real
Italian Chef?
   *No, he's an
impasta.*

Who can write a children's book and give a
great massage at the same time?
   Dr. Masseuse.

What would you get if you crossed a judge
with a surgeon?
   *A person who can get people hitched
   and stitched at the same time.*

Who is the most talkative fairy tale character?

Rap Van Winkle.

What would you get if you crossed a cartoonist with Benedict Arnold?

An Illustraitor.

Why did the two-timing groom cross the road?

To get to the other bride.

What's the difference between a practical joker and a bad friend?

One is always putting you on, the other is always putting you off.

5.
A Mad, Mad World

What kind of cologne did prehistoric man wear?

Aftercave lotion.

Why did the movie star build an ark?

In case he got flooded with fan mail.

Where did the ancient Egyptians bury magicians?

In disa-pyramids.

What do you say when choosing magicians?
"Houdini, meenie, miney, moe..."

What did the sign in Caesar's kitchen say?
"Rome Sweet Rome."

Where does Robin Hood buy flowers for
Maid Marian?
At the Sherwood Florist.

IS THERE A DOCTOR IN THE HOUSE?

What does a sheep say when it sticks its tongue out for the doctor?
"Baaah."

What doctor invented the lightbulb?
Thomas Medicine.

What do doctors say on Halloween?
"Trick or treatment!"

Which one of Adam and Eve's sons was a dentist?
Novo-cain.

What famous painting shows a woman coughing, sneezing, and smiling?
Pneumonia Lisa.

Who handles health club emergencies?
A S.W.E.A.T. team.

What is a surgeon's favorite musical?
Phantom of the Opera-tion.

Who was the hairiest of King Arthur's knights?

Fur Lancelot.

When did knights butt into each other's business?

In the Meddle Ages.

If the children of knights play board games, what do their fathers play?

Sword games.

DID YOU HEAR?

Did you hear the one about the tornado?

Yes, it blew me away.

Did you hear the one about the carpet?

Yes, it had me on the floor.

Did you hear the one about the airplane?

Yes, but it went over my head.

Did you hear the one about the corn field?

Yes, it's the stalk of the town.

What ape helped settle the American frontier?
Daniel Ba-Boone.

What cowboy never said a word?
Quiet Earp.

Who was the smallest cowboy?
Wyatt Twirp.

Who was the funniest cowboy?
Groucho Marksman.

What dog was also a famous explorer?
Barko Polo.

Why did the captain bring the submarine in for repairs?
To replace the shark plugs.

Why didn't the sailor tell the submarine the good news?
So it wouldn't get its scopes up.

What does a sidewalk become when it's icy?
A slidewalk.

What is a slug's motto?
Goo for it.

What do you say when you tickle a slug?
"Coochy, coochy, goo."

What do you say when you tickle a clock?
"Coochy, coochy, cuckoo."

Why are clocks made better and better as time goes on?
Tick-nology improves.

What happens when you irritate a clock?
It gets ticked off.

What do you put on the floor of a baby's room?
Crawl-to-crawl carpeting.

When does a maid work?
From dawn to dust.

What would you get if you crossed an X, an O, and the dog from Oz?
Tick-Tack-Toto.

What did the Kleenex write on the postcard?

"Tissue were here."

What's the difference between a host and a tycoon?

One takes company in, and the other takes companies over.

What would you get if you mixed your mother's red nail polish with her orange nail polish?

In trouble.

If you pay for fruit by the pound, how do you pay for dirt?

By the mound.

What store has the most agreeable salespeople?

O.K.-Mart.

In what part of California do wealthy woodchucks live?

Beaverly Hills.

Do rubber bands lie?

No, they just stretch the truth.

If fish travel in schools, how does thread travel?

In spools.

Who is the smallest dictator?
A ty-runt.

What mouse heads the House of
Representatives?
The Squeaker of the House.

What do dictators wipe their feet on?
Diplo-mats

When do Inuit travel in heavy traffic?
At mush hour.

What state has the most streets?
Road Island.

What city has the most gerbils?
Hamsterdam.

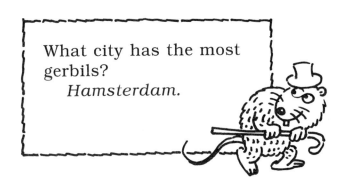

How far is it from one town to the next on an unpaved road?
Just a hop, skip, and a bump.

What's harder than catching a train when you're late?
Throwing one.

What did the riverbed say to the ocean floor?
"My sediments exactly."

Did the pilot fly solo?
No, actually he flew so high.

How do birds measure far distances?
In flight years.

MUDDLED MOTTOES

What's a mechanic's motto?
Oily to bed, oily to rise.

What's a limo driver's motto?
The chauffeur must go on.

What's a housemaid's motto?
Look before you sweep.

What's a baker's motto?
Dough or die.

What's the difference between a star, a suit, and a hose?
One twinkles, one wrinkles, and one sprinkles.

6.
The Scream Team

▼ ▼

Where do monsters learn the cha-cha?
In Dance-ylvania.

What do tourists do in Transylvania?
They go frightseeing.

How can you understand something written in Transylvanian?
Get it Transylated.

How does a one-eyed monster applaud?
It cy-claps.

How does the giant in "Jack and the Beanstalk" hitchhike?
With his Fee Fi Fo thumb.

Was the genie in the magic lamp smart?
Yes, he was a genie-us.

What do you say when choosing a magic lamp?
"Genie, meenie, miney, moe . . ."

Where do giant Eskimos live?
In bigloos.

What monster gets its mouth washed out with soap at every full moon?
A swearwolf.

What duck has two fangs hidden inside its bill?
Count Quackula.

What would you get if you crossed Dracula with a finicky eater?
A vampire that takes one bite and leaves the rest.

What do you get when a monster spills grape juice?
A Franken-stain.

Who helped the Bride of Frankenstein go to the ball?
Her Scary Godmother.

What monster pulls the most practical jokes?
Prankenstein.

When do monsters play practical jokes?
On April Ghouls' Day.

What trick do zombies teach their dogs?
  To play dead.

What do zombies fill with food on warm summer days?
  Picnic caskets.

What's the Creature from the Black Lagoon's favorite dessert?
  Hot sludge sundaes.

How does the Creature from the Black Lagoon score in basketball?
  With a slime dunk.

What do zombie actors drive?
  Re-hearses.

What theory do giggling zombies prove?
  That there is laugh after death.

Was the ghost quiet?
  Yes, it didn't say boo.

WORDS TO THE WILD

What's a zombie's motto?
Die now, play later.

What's an ancient Egyptian grave robber's motto?
Tomb is money.

What did Tinkerbell play with as a young fairy?
Tinker Toys.

How far is it from one tree to the next in a forest?
Just a hop, skip, and a stump.

Who wrote scary stories in rhyme?
Edgar Allan Poet.

What witch writes mysteries?
Hagatha Christie.

How do witches play their records?
In scareo.

What did the winner of the witches' contest receive?
Cursed prize.

What did the witch get when she stayed at the inn?
Broom and board.

If the winner of a contest gets first prize, what does the loser get?

Worst prize.

What's a ghost's favorite cereal?

Eerio's.

What supernatural creature frightens Santa Claus?

The North Pol-tergeist.

Why don't mummies make good friends?

They're too wrapped up in themselves.

Why don't astronauts make good friends?

They're not down to earth.

What is E.T.'s spaceship when he's not in it?

M.T.

What would you get if you crossed E.T. with a cheapskate?

An alien who phones home collect.

Why didn't the Loch Ness Monster answer the door?

It was the serpent's day off.

What does a witch doctor call it when he performs the same magic twice?

Déjà-voo-doo.

How does the Sandman carry his sand?
In a napsack.

What do little Martians learn at camp?
Arts and spacecrafts.

Who does a zombie share its apartment
with?
Its tombmate.

What do you read to little zombies to help
them sleep?
Deadtime stories.

Who represents the views of ghosts?
Their spooksperson.

What race do ghosts love to watch?
Scarathons.

7.
Pun & Games

▼ ▼

Why do owls get invited to so many parties?
Because they're a hoot.

Why are bunnies fun to have at parties?
They hop till they drop.

What's the difference between a generous
host and a snob?
*One puts people up and the other puts
people down.*

What's an amoeba's favorite game?
Divide 'n' seek.

What game do twins love play?
Siamese Says.

What game do boys named Bart like to play?
Simpson Says.

What's a mechanic's favorite card game?
Engine rummy.

What animals make the best poker players?
Bluffalo.

What happened to the zombie after he stayed up all night?
He was dead on his feet.

What do English country gentlemen do on Saturday nights?
Squire dancing.

Do train conductors do the cha-cha?
No, they do the choo-choo.

How do millionaires dance?
Check-to-check.

What kind of music do ogres like?
Rock 'n' troll.

What do insect
ballerinas dance on?
Mosqui-toes.

What kind of music do ancient scribes like?
Rock 'n' scroll.

What kind of music do demolition derby
winners like?
Wreck 'n' roll.

What kind of music do welders like?
Heavy metal.

What kind of music do heroes like?
Heavy medal.

What kind of music do balloons dislike?
Pop music.

What kind of music do convicts dance to?
Rock 'n' Parole

GIVE THEM A BREAK

How do garbage collectors break up with their girlfriends?
They dump them.

How do mountain climbers break up with their girlfriends?
They cut ties.

How do parachutists break up with their boyfriends?
They drop them.

How do amoebas break up with their boyfriends?
They split.

How do ghosts break up with their girlfriends?
They disappear.

How do dogs break up with their girlfriends?
They stop going out.

How do sailors break up with their girlfriends?
They drift apart.

What large stones are used to make costume jewelry?
Rhino-stones.

Who is the most musical deer?
Do-re-mi-fa-so-la-ti-doe.

Who is the silliest singer?
Do-re-mi-fa-so-la-ti-dodo.

What is a druggist's favorite song?
"Old MacDonald Had a Pharmacy."

MOTTO MANIA

What's pantyhose's motto?
Born to run.

What's a hairline's motto?
It's better to give than to recede.

What's Miss Clairol's motto?
Do or dye.

What do you get when you tear a songbook?
Rip music.

What is a Jedi Master's favorite toy?
A yo-yoda.

What do lumberjacks say on Halloween?
"Trick or tree!"

What does a diesel engine say on Halloween?
"Truck or treat!"

What does Captain Picard say on Halloween?

"Trek or treat!"

What amusement park ride is only 12 inches long?

A ruler coaster.

What ride do mothers and babies like?

A stroller coaster.

What's a singer's favorite amusement?

A rock 'n' roller coaster.

8

Classroom Crack-ups

▼ ▼

Why did the little stegosaurus stay home from school?
It had a dino-sore throat.

What do baby architects play with?
City blocks.

What do sailors learn in school?
Their A, B, seas.

What's a farmer's favorite learning game?
Show 'n' Till.

What's the difference between the way students did their homework years ago and the way they do it today?

Years ago students worked on a desk, while today they work on a disk.

What's harder than cutting school?

Gluing it back together.

Do straight-A students get engaged?

Yes, but first they just go study.

What do young bankers learn in school?

How to tell dime.

What do you send to get a message to a geometry teacher?

A parallel-ogram.

Who trains court jesters?

Fool teachers.

How did the wasp do in school?
It had a bee average.

What did the bee study in college?
Buzziness.

What kind of colleges do plants attend?
Ivy League.

How do students know the cost of
education will go up?
In-tuition.

Where do musicians mix chemicals?
In tubas.

How do musicians prepare for exams?
By studying their notes.

What's an English teacher's motto?
Essay come, essay go.

What English course do mummies take in school?
De-composition.

What would you get if you crossed the Big Dipper with a zebra?
Stars and stripes.

What do you call scientists who look for Noah's Ark?
Arkeologists.

Was Ben Franklin surprised when he discovered electricity?
Oh yes, he was shocked!

9

Show Far—Show Good

▼ ▼

How is an actor like a football player?
They both perform plays.

How do actors live life?
One play at a time.

How is a klutz like an actor?
*When a klutz takes a flop, he can end
up in a cast; when an actor is in a cast,
he can end up in a flop.*

What did the director say to the actor with a bad back?

"*Lights, camera, traction!*"

What did the bald actor ask himself?

"*Toupee or not toupee, that is the question.*"

What do superstitious Jedis carry?

Good Luke charms.

What pretty fruit hosts a game show?

Banana White.

Why did Walt Disney go to the mechanic?
For a car-toon up.

What cartoon character is always throwing up?
Barf Simpson.

Who is the most impolite cartoon character?
The Rude-runner.

What do you call a repeat of a Roadrunner cartoon?
A rerun-ner.

How do circus dogs fly through the air?
With the greatest of fleas.

What do animal trainers have when they're too nervous to work?
Cage fright.

What do Moe, Larry, and Curly have when they're too nervous to work?
Stooge fright.

What band can't play music?
A rubber band.

What did the seven dwarfs sing when they worked for Santa Claus?

"Hi ho-ho-ho, hi ho-ho-ho, it's off to work we go . . ."

What would you get if you crossed Miss Piggy with a conceited singer?

A little piggy that sings "me me me" all the way home.

What do fish like to listen to for entertainment?
Sand-up comedy.

What would you get if you crossed a comedian with a boxer?

A comic who knocks you out with his punch line.

How do comedians measure their speed?
In smiles per hour.

What comic team was late for every performance?

Laurel and Tardy.

What comic trio has a Native American in it?

Larry, Curly, and Geronimo.

Where do comedians go when they retire?

To an old jokes home.

What do magicians say to make swarms of hungry insects disappear?

"Locust Pocus."

What is the phone company's favorite musical?

"Phantom of the Opera-tor."

What's the difference between a surfer and a beauty queen?

One floats on top of a wave, the other waves on top of a float.

What Star Trek character has a crooked smile?

Captain Smirk.

What's the difference between constellations and Hollywood?

Nothing—in both, the stars make pictures.

What is the most boring film?
    "Yawn With the Wind."

What movie stars people, cartoon characters, and C3PO?
    "Who Framed Roger Robot?"

What movies do two-headed monsters star in?
    Double creature features.

Who did Charlie Tuna take to the movies?
  His gillfriend.

Who did the tornado take to the movies?
  Its whirlfriend.

What movies make people cry?
  E-motion pictures.

What dog went to Oz to take pictures?
  Phototo.

If Dorothy hadn't found the Tin Man in
time, what might his tombstone have read?
  "Rust in Peace."

What did the cowboy say as Mr. Potato
Head rode off into the sunset?
   "Who was that mashed man?"

10.
Jock Around the Clock

What's a bee's favorite sport?
Sting-pong.

Where do millionaires work out?
At wealth clubs.

How do dogs rap?
Fleastyle.

What kind of attitude does a fisherman need?
Bait 'n' see.

What can run even when you're walking?
Pantyhose.

What does a sweatshirt become when you wear it in the rain?
A wet shirt.

What's the difference between a baseball player and a Boy Scout?
One plays during innings, the other plays
during outings.

What's the difference between a baseball player and a card shark?
One steals bases, the other steals aces.

Why do baseball players make good friends?
They always go to bat for you.

How did the warlock explain his team's no-hitter?
Pitchcraft.

Why can't pitchers make decisions?
They're always changing their mounds.

What did the dugout sampler say?
"Home run sweet home run."

What kind of skirts do basketball players wear?

Hoop skirts.

What's a truck driver's favorite sport?

Clutch football.

Where do high jumpers store their valuables?

In a pole vault.

What do mountaineers do when they're bored?

Climb the walls.

KOOKY CONTESTS

What sport do bananas compete in?
Track and peeled.

What sport do losers compete in?
Track and failed.

What sport do pancakes compete in?
Stack and field.

What sport do dimwits compete in?
Track and fooled.

What would you get if you crossed C3PO with a gymnast?
An ac-robot.

Did you ever ask yourself this silly question: Why does a boxing match have rounds? Shouldn't they be called squares?

What do boxers wear under their uniforms?
Boxer shorts.

What would you get if you crossed an optimist with a boxer?

A fighter who's upbeat even when he's beat up.

Why can't you get a straight answer from wrestlers?

They're hard to pin down.

What kind of foot do you get when you hit it with a golf club?

A swollen-one.

What do you get if you hit a gopher with a golf club?

A mole-in-one.

Where can you hear a cattle roping competition?

On a rodeo station.

How far is it from one basketball court to the next?

Just a hoop, skip, and a jump.

How do you cheer on a basketball player?

"Hoop Hoop Hooray!"

11.

Win Some, Lose Some

▼ ▼

Why don't sticks of dynamite like to race?
They always come in blast place.

Why did the match burn the man?
Because the man struck it first.

What was the heroic daisy awarded?
A petal of honor.

What title did Bullwinkle's beautiful sister win?

Moose Universe.

Why did the gemstone start an argument?
It was tired of being taken for granite.

What would you get if you crossed a gun fighter with a coward?
A cowboy who won't show up for a showdown.

What does a hired hand become when he makes too many mistakes?
A fired hand.

SAY IT AGAIN, SAM

What's a turtle's motto?
All's shell that ends shell.

What's a fish's motto?
Where there's a gill, there's a way.

What's a tailor's motto?
Two threads are better than one.

How do you describe a poor carpet
salesman who became a millionaire?
He went from rugs to riches.

What would you get if you crossed a pauper
with a millionaire?
*A person who can't afford a wallet big
enough for all his money.*

What would you get if you crossed Mary
Sunshine with Gloomy Gus?
*An optimist who always hopes things
will get better, but knows that they won't.*

What illness makes you forget to blow
your nose?

Amsneezia.

What's the difference between the
Terminator and Henny Penny?

One is a warrior, the other is a worrier.

What chicken wrote fairy tales with her
chick?

Hens Christian And-her-son.

Who are the two goofiest nursery rhyme
characters?

Tweedle Dee and Tweedle Dumb-Dumb.

Who is the most boring nursery rhyme
character?

Blah Blah Black Sheep.

Who is a ghost's favorite nursery rhyme character?

Little Boy Boo.

What does Darth Vader take to get from the basement to the roof of his high-rise?

The ele-Vader.

When do hurricanes stop?

Mon-sooner or later.

What's a raindrop's motto?
Two's company, three's a cloud.

What did the horse say when it lost the race?

"Whoa is me!"

What do dogs buy from travel agencies?

Hound trip tickets.

What did the dog say when it was tenth in a 10-dog race?

"Last, but not leashed!"

Index

▼ ▼